Turn Your Dream into Reality

Using Your God-Given Gifts to Fulfill Your Purpose

Melvin L. Taylor Jr.

Copyright © 2019 by **Melvin L. Taylor Jr.**

All rights reserved. No part of this publication may be reproduced, distributed, or transmitted in any form or by any means, without prior written permission.

Unless otherwise specified, Scripture quotations are taken from the New King James Version®. Copyright © 1982 by Thomas Nelson, Inc. Used by permission. All rights reserved.

Scripture quotations marked (MSG) are taken from *The Message*, copyright © 1993, 2002, 2018 by Eugene H. Peterson. Used by permission of NavPress. All rights reserved. Represented by Tyndale House Publishers, Inc.

Scripture quotations marked (NASB) are taken from the New American Standard Bible®, Copyright © 1960, 1962, 1963, 1968, 1971, 1972, 1973, 1975, 1977, 1995 by The Lockman Foundation. Used by permission. www.Lockman.org.

Scripture quotations marked (NIV) are taken from the Holy Bible, New International Version®, NIV® Copyright © 1973, 1978, 1984, 2011 by Biblica, Inc.® Used by permission. All rights reserved worldwide.

Scripture quotations marked (TLB) are taken from The Living Bible copyright © 1971 by Tyndale House Foundation. Used by permission of Tyndale House Publishers, Inc., Carol Stream, Illinois 60188. All rights reserved.

Renown Publishing

Turn Your Dream into Reality / Melvin L. Taylor Jr.
ISBN: 978-1-945793-87-5

This book is dedicated to all who desire to know their purpose, discover their God-given gifts, and turn their dreams into reality.

CONTENTS

You Are Unique 3
PART ONE: The Call to Purpose 5
Get Out of Your Comfort Zone 7
Stepping Out 15
The Process of Purpose 25
The Process of Dreams 33
From Attitude to Altitude 45
PART TWO: The Promise 57
Pregnant with Purpose 59
Your New Season Is Now 69
PART THREE: Discovery of Your Gifts, Purpose, and Dream 81
Living Your Dream 83
Discovering Your Purpose 91
Your Gift, Your Responsibility 103
Release What God Has for You 115
About the Author 117
Notes 119

INTRODUCTION

You Are Unique

> *I will give thanks to You, for I am fearfully and wonderfully made; wonderful are Your works, and my soul knows it very well.*
> —***Psalm 139:14*** *(NASB)*

"Why am I here?"

This question is bound to enter your mind from time to time. You wake up, brush your teeth, eat breakfast, go to work, and come home. Then you do it all over again the next day. On the weekends, you clean, do chores, and run errands. Maybe you go to church on Sunday.

Have you ever stopped to wonder what your purpose is in the midst of all of this routine? Are you longing to live a life of meaning, yet feeling inadequate for the undertaking? Maybe you woke up one day and realized that you're merely going through the motions of everyday life. Maybe that's not enough for you anymore.

Whatever circumstances you find yourself in today, I want to encourage you with this truth: God has a plan for your life, and He has provided you with everything you need to accomplish it.

God has skillfully designed you as a unique individual. There is no one like you, and no one else was born to do what you were created to do. You are a special blessing for someone. Your uniqueness will enable you to do things you never thought possible.

I believe that everyone is born with a purpose and has the opportunity to achieve great things in his or her life. Everyone has the gifts and talents necessary to accomplish his or her purpose. However, not all people know the gifts they possess or understand how to apply them.

This book was written to assist you in discovering your purpose and gifts and putting them into action. There's a workbook section at the end of each chapter that will give you tools to help you discover God's purpose for your life and turn your God-given dream into reality.

Are you ready to learn about your gifts? Are you ready to find true meaning in your life? Are you ready to take hold of a plan that is bigger than anything you've ever imagined?

God has given each of us a dream to do something of significance in the world, something that will make a difference. Instead of sitting on the sidelines, hoping that everything will turn out all right one day, choose to answer God's call and live each day with purpose. You've been given valuable tools to live a meaningful life. You are unique. The world is waiting on you!

PART ONE:
The Call to Purpose

6 · Melvin L. Taylor Jr.

CHAPTER ONE

Get Out of Your Comfort Zone

Sitting on your couch is easy. It's comfortable and safe, and it requires little effort. Reclining in your chair for rest when you're exhausted is fine, but it can also become a problem. The trouble is that resting when you don't truly need to do so can become a bad habit or even a practice of laziness. When you sit around, nothing in your life ever changes. You get frustrated, angry, bored, or complacent, and nothing gets better because you're not doing anything. Nothing's going to change unless you're willing to get out of your comfort zone.

We were not designed to sit around and become comfortable with our routine. We have the opportunity to accomplish greatness. We were born to fulfill a purpose and to make a significant impact in the world. There are many people in various economic situations and seasons of life who have stepped out to accomplish unexpected things.

As the saying goes, "In order to go somewhere you've never gone, you have to do something you've never done." Greatness is inside of you. You have the ability and the resources you need to accomplish what you are meant to do. You were born with potential for the fulfillment of your destiny.

I want to lay the foundation of this book by using one of my favorite characters in the Bible: Abraham, who was originally named Abram.

The Call to Purpose

> Now the LORD had said to Abram: "Get out of your country, from your family and from your father's house, to a land that I will show you. I will make you a great nation; I will bless you and make your name great; and you shall be a blessing. I will bless those who bless you, and I will curse him who curses you; and in you all the families of the earth shall be blessed."
>
> *—Genesis 12:1-3*

Abram was called to leave his country, his family, and his father's house to go to an unknown place with the promise that he would be a great nation and have a great name. God also promised Abram that all of the families of the earth would be blessed as a result of his obedience.

Abram was born in Ur of the Chaldeans. Little is known of his family, but we do know that Terah was his father, Lot was his nephew, and Sarai (who would be renamed Sarah) was his wife.

Terah, Abram, Sarai, and Lot set out for Canaan, but they made a pit stop that lasted much longer than it should have:

> *And Terah took his son Abram and his grandson Lot, the son of Haran, and his daughter-in-law Sarai, his son Abram's wife, and they went out with them from Ur of the Chaldeans to go to the land of Canaan; and they came to Haran and dwelt there. So the days of Terah were two hundred and five years, and Terah died in Haran.*
> —*Genesis 11:31–32*

Terah was on his way to the land of Canaan, but when he arrived at the city of Haran, something distracted him from his assignment, causing him to take his eyes off of the goal. Terah was comfortable in Haran. His wealth overflowed as he grew older. The meaning of *Terah* is "station, or delay."[1] Terah chose to remain in place and delay completion of the journey. He died without ever reaching Canaan. This is an example of what happens when we get stuck in our comfort zone. Purpose can die in the place of delay.

Dr. Myles Munroe said, "The wealthiest place in the world is not the gold mines of South America or the oil fields of Iraq or Iran. [It is] not the diamond mines of South Africa or the banks of the world. The wealthiest place on the planet is just down the road. It is the cemetery. There lie buried companies that were never started, inventions that were never made, bestselling books that were never written, and masterpieces that were never painted. In the cemetery is buried the greatest treasure of untapped potential."[2]

It is vitally important to develop the potential that God has invested in you. Step out of your comfort zone in faith and fulfill your purpose. Do not take your unfulfilled potential down to the grave. Be proactive now.

Do Not Delay

You must get out of the place of delay and complacency and move into the place of purpose. Something great is waiting on you. Sometimes the delay comes from fear of the unknown. Questions arise inside of you: How will I make money? How will my life be different? What steps will I take next?

Abraham was called to give up everything and go to an unknown place, a new land, to start over again. He had to decide whether or not to respond to the call. He had to weigh his options and consider his established lifestyle versus what had been promised to him.

When you are deciding whether or not to follow God's call, it isn't just about you or even your immediate family. The call to something greater is about legacy and generations. It is much bigger than you are.

Abraham gave us a good example of how to overcome challenges, obstacles, and situations that can arise in our lives as we pursue the call to purpose. Even though he was in a place that was intended to delay his purpose, he didn't allow the fear of the unknown to stop him, so don't let it stop you!

WORKBOOK

Chapter One Questions

Question: Describe a time when God called you out of your comfort zone. Did you obey right away or delay? Did you obey completely or only partially? Why were you tempted to hold back?

_____
_____
_____
_____
_____
_____
_____
_____
_____

Question: What are some promises God has given to you? What has He impressed on your heart for your life? Which is stronger: your faith in those promises or your fears? What specific fears hinder your obedience and fuel frustration in your life? What steps can you take to remove that fear and live in faith?

_____
_____
_____
_____
_____
_____
_____
_____
_____
_____

Further Study: Read about the life of Lot in Genesis 11–14 and 19. What factors may have motivated Abraham's unreciprocated loyalty to Lot? How did the men of Sodom attempt to create trouble for Abraham?

_____
_____
_____
_____
_____
_____
_____
_____
_____
_____
_____

Action Step: List the people, places, and things that are familiar to you and make up your comfort zone. Evaluate if any of these people, places, or things are hindering or could hinder you from stepping forward in faith and obedience to God's plan. Ask God to show you how to move beyond those hindrances so you can fulfill His plan for you.

Chapter One Notes

CHAPTER TWO

Stepping Out

So Abram departed as the LORD *had spoken to him, and Lot went with him. And Abram was seventy-five years old when he departed from Haran.*
—***Genesis 12:4***

Abraham's immediate departure is an indication of his faith in God and how he used his measure of faith to develop the gift of faith. Faith entails firm conviction and trust. "It is the divinely implanted principle of inward confidence" in God and all that He has said and done,[3] confidence being trust "based on knowledge or past experience."[4] In essence, confidence "is a measure of how firmly we hold to a particular belief."[5] Faith encompasses belief—and it requires action.

In Abraham's time, leaving family was nearly a death sentence. It meant leaving your safety net. If there was a drought, no one would come with milk and eggs to help you. That's where family came in. Family members shared what they had, helping each other through hard times.

Leaving family was serious in many regards, including the fact that Abraham would probably never see his family again. There were no telephone calls, text messages, or video chats to help them stay connected.

Even with modern communication and transportation, leaving everything one knows and going to a completely unfamiliar place is still difficult. People who are called to serve as missionaries or to take jobs in other states or in foreign countries have to consider stepping out in faith, as Abraham did, when facing such a decision.

Everyone has been given "a measure of faith" (Romans 12:3b). The measure may be different for different people, just as purpose, dreams, and visions are unique to each person. However, no one is without faith. The Bible says that we all have a measure of faith.

Abraham was told that he would be blessed, his people would be blessed, and he would be a great nation. But since he was already wealthy, how much more blessing was he promised?

Note that a vision from God always involves others. A great vision takes more than a leader's lifetime to fulfill. Abraham serves as a prototype of all who seek to have a relationship with God by faith (Hebrews 11:6, 8).

Partial Obedience Is Not Obedience

So Abram departed as the LORD had spoken to him, and Lot went with him.
—Genesis 12:4

Lot was Abraham's nephew, and bringing him along meant that Abraham didn't fully obey the command given to him. Abraham's partial obedience was in direct opposition to God's command because he was to leave his entire family behind, including Lot.

When we partially obey, we are hindering our own purpose and vision. Lot became a hindrance to Abraham, and that could have been avoided if Abraham had chosen to obey completely. The name Lot means "covering," and he was covering the true purpose of Abraham's mission—that Abraham was to be a blessing to all families of the earth.[6]

Picture a veil that covers your head and face, limiting how clearly you can see your surroundings. Lot's presence was like a veil that blocked Abraham's ability to see the vision clearly. Lot's presence would prove to be a major stumbling block in Abraham's journey of purpose.

Note that partial obedience is really disobedience. An example would be if a mother asked her son to wash the dishes before he left the house, and the son took out the garbage but didn't wash the dishes. He did a good thing, but not what was asked of him.

In a similar manner, Abraham departed as the Lord had instructed, but he took Lot with him. Likewise, many people today are doing good things, but not necessarily the God-ordained things that they were born to do. True obedience is immediate and complete.

What's blocking your purpose journey? It may not be a person holding you back. Lot could represent anger, bitterness, unforgiveness, blaming others, and refusing to let go of the past. What's blocking your vision? What's hindering your faith in what God has purposed for your life? Could it be doubt, wrong beliefs, fear, or negative thinking? Whatever is keeping you from seeing God's purpose for you clearly and obeying completely, remove that hindrance so you can walk confidently in God's plan for your life.

Your Faith Will Be Tested

Abraham was about to encounter more problems as a result of his partial obedience.

> Now there was a famine in the land, and Abram went down to Egypt to dwell there, for the famine was severe in the land.
> —***Genesis 12:10***

In a physical sense, famine means lack of food, leading to hunger and starvation. However, for Abraham, it also meant the lack of God's Word in his life. The famine in the land had nothing to do with Abraham, but the fear his father had was attempting to attach itself to Abraham. This fear had the potential to distract Abraham from his calling, causing an unnecessary delay.

Egypt represents a symbol or type of the dependence upon worldly, human resources apart from God. Turning to worldly solutions out of fear is the opposite of faith. A popular acronym for *fear* is False Evidence Appearing Real. Abraham's action showed that he did not trust God to take care of him, his wife, and his servants during this severe famine.

It gets worse. As they were entering Egypt, Abraham's fear of being killed by the Pharaoh of Egypt led him to ask his wife to lie. Abraham assumed that the Egyptians would find Sarah, his wife, so attractive that they would kill him. Abraham told his wife to say that she was his sister so his life would be spared.

Pharaoh invited Sarah to his house, and he treated Abraham well. However, because Pharaoh had taken Abraham's wife, the Lord had to interrupt the situation by causing a plague to come on Pharaoh and his household. Then Pharaoh kicked Abraham and his family out because Abraham had lied to him (Genesis 12:11–20).

Abraham feared that he would die if Sarah didn't lie for him. Remember, fear is the opposite of faith. Fear is your enemy. Its intent is to distract your focus, derail your assignment, and delay your vision—all to stop you from pursuing your purpose. Fear attempts to tell you what you can't do. Fear will cause you to take your eyes off of the prize, the fulfillment of your dreams, vision, and purpose.

In the face of adversity, you have to continue to trust the call to purpose that has been placed in your heart. Proverbs 24:10 says, "You are a poor specimen if you can't stand the pressure of adversity" (TLB). Pressure serves two purposes: it will expose you for who you really are, or it will make you into the leader you were born to be.

Abraham went to Egypt to hide from his purpose. He made an excuse and took a detour. Fear caused him to hide from his call, and doubt caused him to deviate from his purpose. Abraham put other people's lives in jeopardy as a result of his fear. Our decisions affect others. Abraham sometimes failed, yet he is ultimately remembered as a man of faith (Romans 4; Galatians 3:6–9, 26–29).

If you have been struggling with fear, there is hope for you. You have to move beyond the place of fear and begin to move into the place of purpose by faith.

WORKBOOK

Chapter Two Questions

Question: In your own words, how would you define faith? In whom or what do you put your faith?

_____
_____
_____
_____
_____
_____
_____
_____
_____
_____

Question: How does trusting God to provide for you free you from fear and worry?

_____
_____
_____
_____
_____
_____
_____
_____
_____
_____

Further Study: Read Genesis 12:10–20. Why did God protect Abraham even when he was faithless and deceptive?

_____
_____
_____
_____
_____
_____

_____

_____

_____

_____

_____

Action Step: Looking back through this chapter, make a bulleted list of the reasons why it is vital to have faith in order to operate within your purpose.

Chapter Two Notes

CHAPTER THREE

The Process of Purpose

Then Abram went up from Egypt, he and his wife and all that he had, and Lot with him, to the South. Abram was very rich in livestock, in silver, and in gold. And he went on his journey from the South as far as Bethel, to the place where his tent had been at the beginning, between Bethel and Ai, to the place of the altar which he had made there at first. And there Abram called on the name of the LORD.
—***Genesis 13:1–4***

Trust God, and your promises will be delivered. The journey continues when you agree to follow the process of purpose in obedient submission to the plan of God. If you get off track, the best thing to do is to go back to the place where you first heard God speak to you concerning the vision.

Genesis 12:7 tells us that the Lord appeared to Abraham to confirm what He had promised. Then Abraham moved on and pitched his tent, built an altar, and called on the name of the Lord. This happened prior to the severe famine that derailed Abraham's faith. When Abraham left

Egypt, he went back to the place where he had spoken to God to realign himself with his assignment.

I am convinced that this prayer was different from Abraham's previous prayer. I believe that Abraham was asking God to search his heart to see if there was anything wicked in him, as David did in Psalm 139:23–24. Wickedness may be lurking in the recesses of our hearts. Self-judgment is better than vengeance, and it should be done in the presence of God through prayer.

Sometimes you will have to go back to the place of prayer where you heard from God concerning the vision in order to refresh the vision and learn from your mistakes. You will make some mistakes along the way. You will also have some delays based on your decisions or other circumstances. The only way to move on in purpose is to learn from your failures.

Let It Go

God called Abraham to leave his country, his family, and his father's house. In order to make Abraham and his descendants a great nation that would bring blessings to all of the families of the earth, God had to separate Abraham from all that was familiar to him, including his idolatrous family (Joshua 24:2–3). It's possible that Terah received the original call to go to the promised land but failed to complete the assignment. It could be that he was distracted by the spirit of the other gods he served.

Remember, partial obedience is disobedience. In order to go to the place of promise, you must pray according to your purpose to see where you are and to receive clarity about what God is calling you to do.

Abraham set out as the Lord instructed him, but he took Lot with him, which he was not supposed to do. Lot brought problems, strife, and stress. It's time to let Lot go! Separate yourself from people, places, and things that are blocking your purpose, vision, and promise.

It wasn't until Abraham separated himself from Lot that he was able to see the promise of God (Genesis 13:8–18). After Lot left, God said to Abram, "Lift your eyes now and look from the place where you are—northward, southward, eastward, and westward; for all the land which you see I give to you and your descendants forever" (Genesis 13:14–15).

Clarity of your vision and purpose comes when you remove the cover from your eyes. You need to be free of distractions and spiritual contaminants. You can't obtain the promises of God in a place of disobedience. Your purpose journey can continue only when you search your heart through prayer and detach yourself from anything that could inhibit your pursuit of purpose.

If you're not focused, it's easy to get distracted, kick back, and relax all day in the place of comfort and delay. It's easy to allow stagnation to creep into your life because of the fear of letting go of familiar things. But if you dare to step out in faith and obedience, the blessings will flow enough to keep you going, even through the hard times.

Abraham followed through on his commitments. He didn't make the same mistake that his father made. However, he did make some mistakes. His ability to remain focused was vital to his success, in spite of his shortcomings.

Traits of Godly Leaders

Abraham showed three traits of godly leadership that we can apply to our lives. First, Abraham had faith to take risks. Godly leaders are willing to risk everything on God's faithfulness and to venture into the unknown.

Second, Abraham had faith to trust. Godly leaders do not rely on facts alone. They go beyond facts to faith and prayer. Abraham said to his nephew, Lot, "Is not the whole land before you? Please separate from me. If you take the left, then I will go to the right; or, if you go to the right, then I will go to the left" (Genesis 13:9). It didn't matter to Abraham which direction he chose. He only knew that he needed to separate himself from what had become a distraction to him as a result of his disobedience.

According to the next verse, "Lot lifted his eyes and saw all the plain of Jordan, that it was well watered everywhere…" (Genesis 13:10). Lot chose for himself what looked good, but Abraham chose what was good because he knew what God had promised him. Everything that glitters is not gold. Godly leaders don't rely on how attractive things may look or seem. Instead, they rely on what God has purposed for their lives.

Finally, Abraham had faith to surrender. The godly leader is willing to sacrifice all things precious in order to please God. You have to be willing to surrender your desires, your plans, and your life to God if you are going to fulfill your purpose and inherit the promise.

WORKBOOK

Chapter Three Questions

Question: Have you ever gone off track from how God wants you to live or something He asked you to do? What derailed you? How can you learn from your mistakes and failures?

_____
_____
_____
_____
_____
_____
_____
_____
_____
_____

Further Study: Read Genesis 12:1–20, 17:1–27, and 22:1–19 and take note of the qualities or traits of a leader. How can you incorporate these traits into your life?

Action Step: Pray to God and ask Him to search your heart. Ask Him to reveal to you any wickedness that may be keeping you from obeying His instructions fully. Make a list of everything you need to let go of in order to follow God with a pure heart and clarity of purpose, and begin making those changes today.

Chapter Three Notes

32·Melvin L. Taylor Jr.

CHAPTER FOUR

The Process of Dreams

After these things the word of the Lord came to Abram in a vision, saying, "Do not be afraid, Abram. I am your shield, your exceedingly great reward."
—*Genesis 15:1*

The process of vision happens in time. Ecclesiastes 3:1 tells us, "To everything there is a season, a time for every purpose under heaven." There is a time for everything and a season of life for every purposed activity to manifest on the earth.

A season is a period of the year that is distinguished by special climate conditions. There are four temperate seasons we experience: spring, summer, fall, and winter. Each season has its own particular weather patterns that repeat yearly, as well as activities we associate with it.

In the spring, leaves appear on the trees, the grass grows green, flowers begin to bloom, and the fields are planted with seeds for crops. Some crops may be ready for harvest in only a few weeks, while others may not be ready until many months later.

Many people relax during the summer months. With the kids out of school, families take vacations. People have cookouts and go to the beach. Also, throughout the summer, crops become ready for harvest.

In the fall, students and teachers return to school. The weather is cooler, and the leaves begin to change colors. In the Northern Hemisphere, September is when most grains and other spring-planted crops are harvested. Fruit crops, like apples and grapes, are also harvested in the fall.

Sometimes after a field is harvested, farmers plow it and add more fertilizer. This helps to restore nutrients in the soil that the last crop depleted. Then the farmers begin planting some crops for the next year.

In the winter, farmers reflect on the past year and make plans for the next season. They make repairs to the farm equipment, buildings, and tools. These need to be ready in time for spring and the new growing season.

Our lives also go through seasons. Depending on what season of life we may be in, the activities to be done vary. You may wonder why it seems like your vision is taking a long time to come to pass. You may be in a season of preparation or planting instead of a season of harvesting. Furthermore, your vision is not just about you. There are other people connected to you or who will be recipients of the vision. Even if you think that you're ready, you may need to wait for God to get other people ready.

It takes patience, dedication, and commitment for your dream to become a reality and manifest itself. Remember, there is a proper time for everything. While you are waiting for your vision to be realized, you must live a focused life of faith and continue to walk in your purpose every day.

According to Ecclesiastes 3:11, "He [God] has made everything beautiful in its time. He has also set eternity in the human heart; yet no one can fathom what God has done from beginning to end" (NIV).

Therefore, the process of purpose and dreams is to continue to exercise your faith, maximize your gifts, stay focused on your purpose, and add value to others, knowing that in the fullness of time, your vision shall come to fruition.

God's Vision, Our Vision

Genesis 15:1 states, "After these things the word of the LORD came to Abram in a vision." The word *vision* here refers to a divine, often prophetic or revelatory message from God.[7] The vision Abraham received was a word from the Lord: "Do not be afraid, Abram. I am your shield, your exceedingly great reward" (Genesis 15:1).

As I mentioned in an earlier chapter, fear is the enemy of our faith. Fear is always present. Even though Abraham had conquered some of his fears and had separated himself from familiar things, he was still dealing with fearful thoughts of doubt concerning his future and the promises of God.

However, God did not want Abraham to be afraid, and He doesn't want us to be afraid, either. As Paul wrote, "For God has not given us a spirit of fear, but of power and of love and of a sound mind" (2 Timothy 1:7). God knew about Abraham's fear, just as He knows what is on your mind, so He sent His word to Abraham in a vision.

Abraham attempted to defend his case, stating his concern about the fact that he was childless (Genesis 15:2–3). Here again, the Lord took him outside and said, "Look now toward heaven," and reminded him of the promise (Genesis 15:5). Abraham's silence was a way of giving credence to God's word: "And he believed in the LORD, and He accounted it to him for righteousness" (Genesis 15:6). God's way always has been and always will be for His people to trust in His word, which produces right living.

I believe that each of us has a vision placed so deep inside the heart that it speaks to the soul. The vision is the beginning of our journey to finding and fulfilling what we were born to do. Our vision and dreams are linked to our purpose, and our vision requires the use of our faith.

Dreams and Vision

A vision from God, as I've mentioned, is a prophetic message. It is a revelation that comes through insight from God. God-given dreams are spiritual experiences rooted deep in our hearts, never to be forgotten.

According to Genesis 15:12–16, while Abraham was in a deep sleep, God informed him of the future through a dream. God revealed to Abraham that his descendants would be afflicted in a foreign land for four hundred years. The nation Abraham's people would serve would be judged by God, and Abraham's descendants would leave with many possessions. Abraham would die at an old age.

Then God made a covenant with Abraham (Genesis 15:17–21). God humbled Himself to accept the role of the inferior party of the covenant by walking between the bleeding pieces of split animals, as one taking an oath of loyalty to his superior. This dramatic act prefigures the precious gift of His own Son, who would die on a degrading cross for all humanity. The Lord's promise to Abraham was unconditional, and Abraham simply believed.

In 1989, the Lord gave me a daytime dream in which I was on a large platform, walking back and forth, ministering to multitudes of people. It was an open-air setting. I call the vision "a church without walls" because I didn't see any structures on the side or above my head, only a sea of people.

As I was preaching the gospel, many people were getting saved, receiving deliverance from all kinds of bondages, and being healed from all manner of diseases. There were people on the platform with me who were playing instruments and singing songs to the Lord, while others were praying with people in the crowd.

Later that year, the Lord gave me a word from the book of Joshua:

> *Every place that the sole of your foot will tread upon I have given you, as I said to Moses. ... Be strong and of good courage, for to this people you shall divide as an inheritance the land which I swore to their fathers to give them.*
> *—Joshua 1:3, 6*

I believe that this word from the Lord described the assignment for my life. God called me to pastor a group of people. I was to teach them how to discover their God-given purpose, equip them for the work of ministry, and train them to reach the lost, broken, and downtrodden with the gospel of Jesus Christ. By this we will possess our inheritance as promised by God Almighty.

Trusting God's Plan

It doesn't matter how old or young you are because God has set the right time for your dreams and vision, as He did for Abraham. Abraham wanted a son, but he was old. God told Abraham that He would give him a son (Genesis 15:4, 17:16, 17:19). Abraham initially doubted God's promise and took matters into his own hands.

He had a son with his wife's servant (Genesis 16:1–4, 15–16), which led to trouble in the future and delayed the promise. Abraham leaned on his own understanding instead of waiting on God's timing to fulfill the dream, but he learned from his mistake and renewed his faith in God's promise.

Sometimes, like Abraham, we get impatient when we can't see how the dream will be accomplished. However, we have to submit to God's timing. If He gave us the dream to do something great, He will see it through. Our responsibility is "to walk worthy of the calling" (Ephesians 4:1).

"Walk" does not refer to taking a stroll. It means to stay in step with the Lord, to move precisely as He moves. When God acts, you act. When He pauses, you pause. As you walk in sync with the Lord, you will find that the path He takes is always the right way and His timing is always the right time. When you walk with the Lord, you can be sure to get the right results.

One morning, I came before the Lord in prayer to ask for wisdom concerning my life. At that particular time, I had a lot of things going on that I felt were pulling me away from my personal time with the Lord and interfering with the development of the ministry and time with my family. I believed that I was doing what the Lord had ordered for my life, but I was overwhelmed and uncomfortable with this.

In my brief prayer of asking for forgiveness and wisdom, I sensed the Lord leading me to read my devotional for the day. As I obeyed and opened the book to the date of my specific reading, I saw that the title of the devotion was "Stay in Step with God." The Scripture reading was Ephesians 2:10: "For we are His workmanship, created in Christ Jesus for good works, which God prepared beforehand that we should walk in them."

The devotion said that you must never think you can compartmentalize your life based on categories, seasons, or circumstances, because you are not operating on your own. Rather, you are operating according to the plans and power of God within you.

Some things may feel uncomfortable to you, and you may wonder if the things that challenge you are in line with your purpose. You may consider taking matters into your own hands, but don't! The Lord will always lead you in the right direction to get His results out of your life at the right time. As Proverbs tells us, "A man's heart plans his way, but the LORD directs his steps" (Proverbs 16:9).

The Beginning of Greatness

I believe that every person has the opportunity to be a leader, and I believe that every leader has a dream for a better future. God-given dreams are the beginning of greatness. How you move forward from here is the journey, the process of becoming the person God created you to be. As your dream comes together, it will explode into the world, making a significant impact.

You need to exercise your dream. Act on it so that it will not become stagnant. If you want to play the piano well, you need to practice and keep practicing. The only way to realize your dream is to act on it and develop yourself in order to become the leader you were born to be.

Leaders are determined to make the dream a reality. Leaders call others to follow them toward a better way. People are watching you to see how you handle life. Your attitude matters, as we'll see in the next chapter.

WORKBOOK

Chapter Four Questions

Question: What is the difference between dreams and a vision? Have you received a dream or vision from God? How do you know? Does your dream align with your purpose?

_____
_____
_____
_____
_____
_____
_____
_____
_____

_____

_____

Question: Why is God's timing important in the process of dreams being fulfilled?

_____

_____

_____

_____

_____

_____

_____

_____

Further Study: Read the story of the life of Abraham. At each unexpected twist and turn, how did he continue to hold on to the promise of God? How can you tell that he never gave up faith? How do you continue to keep the faith during seasons of difficulty and times of waiting?

_____

_____

_____
_____
_____
_____
_____
_____
_____
_____

Action Step: What can you do to prepare yourself for turning your dream into reality?

Chapter Four Notes

CHAPTER FIVE

From Attitude to Altitude

You may be familiar with the story of the tortoise and the hare[8], but there is something we can learn from the story that you may not have considered before.

The hare knew that he was fast. To mock the slow tortoise, the hare challenged him to a race. The tortoise accepted.

On race day, crowds gathered to watch. The hare was confident of victory. When the race began, the hare bounded forth while the tortoise plodded slowly from the starting line. The hare had a strong lead and kept getting farther ahead. He was sure that the race was in the bag, so he stopped for a quick nap.

The hare awoke just in time to hear cheering as the tortoise crossed the finish line. The hare was faster, but he had the wrong attitude. While the tortoise was slower, his attitude was steady, and he won.

How high you rise in life isn't about your education, intelligence, talent, or ability; it's about your attitude. An attitude is a way of thinking or feeling about something or someone, including oneself. A person's attitude determines the way he or she perceives life, and it shows in his or her behavior.

How we think and what we think about affect us mentally, physically, and emotionally. According to researchers, the majority of illnesses that plague us today are a direct result of an unhealthy thought life. Approximately 75 to 98 percent of all mental, physical, and emotional illness comes from our thought life.[9]

We need to stop falling for the devil's lies and learn how to use our minds correctly. Your mind has the ability to change things. You have creative power because you were created in God's image and according to His likeness (Genesis 1:26–27; Psalm 139:14).

Attitude Adjustment

We develop healthy thoughts when we read, pray about, and meditate on God's Word daily and do what it says. When we don't do what the Word says, we get negative results. God said to Joshua:

> *This Book of the Law shall not depart from your mouth, but you shall meditate in it day and night, that you may observe to do according to all that is written in it. For then you will make your way prosperous, and then you will have good success.*
> —*Joshua 1:8*

Developing a positive attitude is critical for the fulfillment of your dreams and vision. Cultivating the right attitude involves meditation, observation, and action. Meditate on what God has said to you through His Word and actively recite in your mind what He has told you regarding your purpose, assignment, and dream. If you focus and reflect on God's Word and His will for you, it will help to protect you from distractions and negative thoughts that bombard your mind.

Mind Control

For as he thinks in his heart, so is he.
—Proverbs 23:7

Much of our thinking is habitual. If we think about God and good things, godly thoughts become natural. Whatever we focus our thoughts on the most will become part of our belief system. The areas where we put our energies and our attention are the things that will develop in our lives. Our thoughts will stir our emotions, and we will make the decision to follow them.

Thousands of thoughts flow through our minds daily. If we don't control them, our minds become the battleground of our enemy, who will initiate his evil plan for us through our thoughts. Negative thinking leads to negative assumptions, which may lead to negative self-talk. You may even question God's calling, doubting that you have what it takes to do something, to talk about something, to deliver a message to somebody. If you are not careful, you will talk yourself out of the blessings God has for you.

If we focus on what we are not or what we haven't

accomplished, we are allowing the devil to keep us bound. Negative thoughts are the fuel for discouragement, depression, and many other negative emotions. If we focus only on the negative things in our lives, we become negative people. We create most of our problems by choosing to think about things that are contrary to what God has said about us!

Start with the Heart

When facing great challenges, do not allow your mind to dwell on negative thoughts, and do not allow your mouth to speak unbelieving or demoralizing words. Second Corinthians 10:5 tells us to "demolish arguments and every pretension that sets itself up against the knowledge of God, and ... take captive every thought to make it obedient to Christ" (NIV).

We cannot control everything we see and hear. However, our refusal to think negative thoughts and speak words of doubt and fear will keep our hearts inclined to what God has said. We will dwell on what He will do in our lives rather than on what we cannot do. Proverbs 4:20–23 encourages us along similar lines:

> *My son, give attention to my words; incline your ear to my sayings. Do not let them depart from your eyes; keep them in the midst of your heart; for they are life to those who find them, and health to all their flesh. Keep your heart with all diligence, for out of it spring the issues of life.*

Give God's Word your full attention. How? "Incline

your ear" (Proverbs 4:20) to God's Word and keep your eyes focused on it. Be careful what you listen to, because it will determine how you see yourself and your vision (Mark 4:24). Keep God's Word "in the midst of your heart" (Proverbs 4:21). Your heart is the control center of your beliefs. Protect your mind by filtering what goes into your heart, because whatever is in your heart will determine the outcome of your life.

Through meditating on the Word, you will increase your knowledge and understanding of God and your life. According to Proverbs 20:27, "The spirit of a man is the lamp of the LORD, searching all the inner depths of his heart." All of your thoughts, desires, words, and actions flow from your inner being, deep within your heart. If you look into the Word as into a mirror, it will identify areas of your life that need some work.

Positive Change

The next step in developing a positive attitude is to apply what you have learned through observation of yourself. Pray and ask God for His help to accomplish your goals for change. As you focus on improving yourself by applying the Word to your life daily, "you will make your way prosperous" and "have good success" in life (Joshua 1:8).

Positive self-worth is a prime characteristic of a person with a good attitude. People who do not believe in themselves expect the worst not only of themselves, but also of others. People with low self-confidence struggle to focus on anything but themselves because they are always concerned with how they look, what others think of them, and whether they are going to fail.

A lot of people are afraid of failing. We are going to make mistakes because of sin. However, through life in Christ, it's been predetermined that we will always win as long as we keep our eyes on Jesus, "the author ... of our faith" (Hebrews 12:2), and we learn from our failures. We must go through all trials with the right attitude. We will experience some failures, only to realize who we are and what we already have in Him.

Forging a Leader

Before God could use Abraham, he had to be prepared, purified, and forged into the leader he had the potential to become. The same is true for you. Everyone must go through a process of progress.

We need time to mature, to grow in ways that enable us to handle the work that has been prepared for us. Abraham received the vision at seventy-five years old and finally completed his assignment at 175 years old. There were twenty-five years of preparation from the time of the call to the birth of the promised son, and then Abraham lived another seventy-five years in promise as "the father of a multitude of nations" (Genesis 17:4–5 NASB).

During the time of growth, we must face challenges, obstacles, and difficulties. Great leaders are formed only through trials (Romans 5:1–5). Remember, diamonds are created under extreme pressure. The same is true of leaders. When faced with adversity, people become either bitter or better. You must allow your trials to strengthen and prepare you for the dream God has for you.

James wrote:

> *My brethren, count it all joy when you fall into various trials, knowing that the testing of your faith produces patience. But let patience have its perfect work, that you may be perfect and complete, lacking nothing.*
> —*James 1:2–4*

Only through testing do we discover our character and reach maturity in the faith. Romans 4:13–22 describes the testing of Abraham's faith. When the pressure is on and you are called to put your faith in God when His promised outcome looks unlikely or impossible, that's when you will discover what your values are. How you respond to testing reveals your true character.

You may face several tests. Abraham remained true to God as he experienced a variety of personal challenges. God could not use Abraham until he had been tested and proven. Don't be dismayed if it seems that you are going through one trial after another. Don't be afraid that God has let you down. It is all part of the process. Abraham learned to lead under difficult circumstances, and you will as well.

God must orchestrate this process of testing and growth. Without God, a leader can do nothing of real value (John 15:5). Your relationship with God comes first. If you are walking in obedience to Him, you can be sure that He is directing the process and will bring you through it.

The Power of Attitude

John Maxwell said, "A dream together with a positive attitude produces a person with unlimited possibilities and potential."[10] Having the right attitude will take you where you dream of going. No matter the circumstances, positive people understand that opportunities are the result of having the right attitude. It is imperative that you develop a positive perspective to carry you through the process of reaching your dreams.

Positive change will not happen unless you're willing to step forward and take full responsibility for your thoughts and actions. The Bible tells us to take our thoughts captive (2 Corinthians 10:5). Our thoughts lead to words, and we are responsible for all of the idle words we speak (Matthew 12:36).

Taking responsibility for your thoughts and words is a step toward taking responsibility for your actions and identifying areas where you need improvement. When you take responsibility for yourself, you open yourself up in humility to the transforming work of the Holy Spirit. It is only then that you can be shaped and molded for what God has planned.

WORKBOOK

Chapter Five Questions

Question: Proverbs 23:7 teaches that what you think shapes who you are. Do you look for the good in others or assume the worst? Are you a giver or a taker in your relationships?

_____
_____
_____
_____
_____
_____
_____
_____
_____
_____

Question: In what ways have you experienced testing of your faith? What did you learn and how did you grow through these difficult times and challenging situations?

Further Study: How did Abraham exemplify a positive attitude?

_____

_____

_____

_____

_____

_____

_____

Action Step: Begin making changes today to eliminate negativity from your life.

Chapter Five Notes

PART TWO:
The Promise

CHAPTER SIX

Pregnant with Purpose

> *But My covenant I will establish with Isaac, whom Sarah shall bear to you at this set time next year.*
> *—Genesis 17:21*

When God promised Abraham a son, he believed Him (Genesis 15:4–6). Years went by, and Abraham and Sarah still had no children. They were getting old, and their faith was exhausted. They decided to take matters into their own hands.

Sarah suggested that Abraham should try to have children by her maidservant Hagar, since Sarah was barren. Abraham agreed to do what his wife said (Genesis 16:1–4).

Sarah illustrates the danger of taking God's promises into your own hands. If you are not careful to trust God, you may make extra trouble for yourself and suffer consequences that you did not foresee. Proverbs 19:21 tells us, "Many are the plans in a person's heart, but it is the LORD's purpose that prevails" (NIV).

The Full Picture

Abraham received the vision of God through a dream, and he believed the promise of God in his heart. However, instead of trusting God's plan completely, Abraham and his wife thought that it was taking God too long to do what He had said. They decided to help Him along, since, according to Sarah, God kept her from having children (Genesis 16:2).

The truth is that Sarah's lack of faith kept her from having a child. Faith is not based on what we see with the natural eye: "For we walk by faith, not by sight" (2 Corinthians 5:7). Faith is based on what we believe in our hearts concerning the things God has promised us. It is "the substance of things hoped for, the evidence of things not seen" (Hebrews 11:1).

Faith is essential to our relationship with God. Hebrews 11:6 tells us that "without faith it is impossible to please Him, for he who comes to God must believe that He is, and that He is a rewarder of those who diligently seek Him." We have to stay true to our faith if we are going to see the purpose and vision God has given us come to pass, and that includes trusting God's timing. God knew the end from the very beginning of time. He sees the entire plan for our lives from start to finish. If anyone knows how to get the timing right, it's God.

When an architect sits down to plan, he considers the landscape and then starts to work on drawings. He goes through multiple revisions until a plan is approved. Soon someone posts a sign of the building's architectural drawing on a vacant lot. The drawing shows detailed landscapes, the design and color of the building, the windows, and even a projected date for when the building will be finished.

The detailed picture of what the completed building will look like gives the public confidence in the purpose of the building because the picture reveals what is to come. There's not only assurance of an expected outcome, but also excitement about what's coming.

We can't see all that God has planned for our lives. We must discover the details along the way and trust God for the end result. Proverbs 3:5–6 says, "Trust in the LORD with all your heart, and lean not on your own understanding; in all your ways acknowledge Him, and He shall direct your paths."

God wants us to fulfill our purpose and successfully complete our journey, and He wants us to trust Him to get us there. He doesn't want us to be concerned with how He is going to do what He said He would do. Instead of falling back into our old ways of doing things based on our own efforts, we need to have faith that God will provide for us in the right way and at the right time.

Change of Name, Change of Character

> *No longer shall your name be called Abram, but your name shall be Abraham; for I have made you a father of many nations.*
> —***Genesis 17:5***

Abraham tried to hurry God's promise along by having a son by Hagar, but God's plan was still in motion according to His will. God told Abraham that he would have the son of the promise by his wife, Sarah, in a year (Genesis 17:15–21). At that point, Sarah was ninety years old, and Abraham was nearly a hundred years old.

God changed Abram's name to Abraham as a sign that His promise would come to pass (Genesis 17:1–8). Abram means "exalted father," and Abraham means "father of a multitude" (Genesis 17:5, footnotes). Every time Abraham heard his name spoken, he was reminded of the promise and of who he was.

The change of name represented a change of character. Abraham's new name shaped his concept of himself. Let God's words, which designate His will and promise for your life, become fixed in your mind. Let them govern your speech. Do not identify yourself as anything less than what God calls you.

As a teenager, my nickname was Mellow. I didn't like my name because I didn't think that the name Melvin was fitting for my personality. *Mellow* means calm and relaxed or pleasantly soft. People who knew me back then know that *mellow* did not at all describe my character at the time. When I gave my life to the Lord, however, I started using my birth name, which in Gaelic refers to a chief.

When I was a young boy, I wanted to be an attorney to defend people, as a good chief defends and protects his people. Due to circumstances in life, I was unable to obtain the professional status of an attorney, but because my purpose had already been determined by God, He called me to be one of the generals in His army to war on behalf of His people. Now, here I am, writing to you about understanding your purpose, discovering your God-given gifts, and turning your dreams into reality.

Timing Is Everything

> *And the LORD visited Sarah as He had said, and the LORD did for Sarah as He had spoken. For Sarah conceived and bore Abraham a son in his old age, at the set time of which God had spoken to him. ... Now Abraham was one hundred years old when his son Isaac was born to him.*
> *—Genesis 21:1-2, 5*

God's plans will not always make sense to us. By human reasoning, God's timing for Abraham and Sarah to have a son was way off. Abraham was a hundred years old, and Sarah had left her childbearing years behind her. And yet, God gave them a son, just as He had said He would.

You may think that God is taking too long to come through on the dreams He has given you. You may think that the opportunity has passed, but God's plans and His timing are always exactly right. Whether you know it or not, there are some specific things God planned for you before you were born (Jeremiah 1:5).

If you trust and obey God, then everything in your life will lead you to the point of receiving His purpose and plan for you. Don't lose faith or try to make things happen apart from God's will. Instead of worrying about present circumstances or the future, reflect on how God has provided for you in the past and look for encouragement in His Word.

There is a set time for the manifestation of your vision

and fulfillment of your purpose. The time may not come as quickly as you want it to come, but it will come. The steps to arrive there may not unfold as you expect them to unfold, but they will take you where God wants you to go. God is capable of the impossible, and He will come through powerfully for those who trust in Him.

WORKBOOK

Chapter Six Questions

Question: Have you ever been frustrated with God's timing? Did you decide to wait on the Lord or take matters into your own hands? What was the result?

_____
_____
_____
_____
_____
_____
_____
_____
_____
_____

Question: Find out the meaning of your name and write the definition below. How does your name reflect or influence your character? How would you define yourself? How does your view of yourself compare to how God defines you?

_____

_____

_____

_____

_____

_____

_____

_____

_____

Further Study: Read Habakkuk 2:2–4 and make note of key points that stand out to you. How does the passage relate to our discussion in this chapter?

_____

_____

_____

_____

_____

_____

_____

_____

_____

_____

_____

Action Step: What changes are you eager for God to make in your life? What promises are you excited for God to fulfill? Consider the practical ways you can exercise the principle of waiting on the Lord's timing.

Chapter Six Notes

CHAPTER SEVEN

Your New Season Is Now

The next season in your life is about releasing things that God has promised you. However, the next season is not next year. You must start tomorrow morning.

God's plan for you may require you to make changes in your personal life. Don't put off obeying God or hold on to what He tells you to leave behind. I want to give you practical steps to move forward and walk into your next season.

Submission to God

God requires us to be in submission to His plans for our lives. It's helpful to think of the word *submission* as comprising two words. The prefix *sub-* indicates "under" or "below," and we use the noun *mission* to refer to a specific assignment on which someone is sent. Combined, we can think of the word *submission* as placing yourself under God's authority, which implies obedience to the tasks He assigns to you. Submission will require you to give up the things you love dearly for a cause greater than you.

Faith is required for us to come under the mission of God. Abraham finally had his son against all odds. He had endured quite a few trials to get to that point. Then God gave Abraham the hardest test of faith: "Take now your son, your only son Isaac, whom you love, and go to the land of Moriah, and offer him there as a burnt offering on one of the mountains of which I shall tell you" (Genesis 22:2).

Abraham took Isaac into the mountains, but just before he was going to sacrifice Isaac, God stopped Abraham and provided another sacrifice, a ram in the bush (Genesis 22:3–14). The timely intervention of God foreshadowed God offering "His only begotten Son," Jesus, to die in our place as a sacrifice to save humanity (John 3:16).

Your God-given vision must die in order for it to come to pass. You have to be willing to give your dream back to God, and then He will resurrect the vision He has given you (Proverbs 16:1–3).

Our thoughts, perceptions, and reasonings stop us from truly surrendering to God. We have to crucify the thoughts of fear in our minds (2 Corinthians 10:4–5; Romans 12:2). Philippians 4:8 says that we should think—and not think randomly, but in a focused and purposeful way—about things that are pure and praiseworthy.

We are always thinking about something, whether it be good or bad, positive or negative. Even when we go to sleep at night, our minds are still working, thinking about things we did during the day. We think twenty-four hours a day, seven days a week.

Nothing is more important than a thought. Your

thoughts about yourself determine who you are and who you will become. Remember what Proverbs 23:7 tells us: "as he thinks in his heart, so is he." What we think, we believe, and belief is in the heart. If we don't have good thoughts about ourselves, then it's impossible to have faith to believe that we can accomplish anything of greatness.

Thinking on your purpose will require you to take control of your thoughts by not allowing random, negative thoughts to run through your mind. Philippians 4:8 tells us how to take charge of what we think. You need to think on things that are in line with God's nature, His will, and the vision He gives you.

Take hold of these principles and apply them to your life. God tested Abraham, and you will be tested, too. Times of testing are not meant to defeat you, but to prove and refine your faith and help you see who you are.

Sensitivity to God's Voice

Early in the morning, Abraham took his son Isaac, two servants, and the wood for the burnt offering and set off to the place where God had told him to go to sacrifice his son (Genesis 22:3). You have to see the place of promise through the eyes of faith, just as Abraham "saw the place afar off" (Genesis 22:4). You may not be able to see it right in front of your eyes for a while. However, results will be revealed as you listen to and obey God's voice.

John 10:27 tells us that God's people hear His voice and follow Him. We come to know the voice of God through spending time in His Word and in prayer.

There are many voices in this world. Many people won't understand your dream and will question you, but you must be sensitive to God's voice. He will give you comfort and direction concerning your vision, dreams, and purpose.

Hope Against All Odds

Notice that Abraham didn't tell anyone about his orders from God (Genesis 22:3–8). How could he? How would anyone else understand the test God was giving him? Usually, the faith test must be withstood alone. Sometimes you have to separate yourself from people for a season while you are on a God-focused assignment.

Not everyone will go where you are going. Not everyone will be able to handle what you have to undertake to accomplish your dream. Some people may even try to prevent you from achieving your purpose, simply because not everyone understands what it takes to fulfill the assignment you have been given.

Abraham told his servants, "Stay here with the donkey while I and the boy go over there. We will worship and then we will come back to you" (Genesis 22:5 NIV). Notice how Abraham's faith is evident in his words. Abraham said, "We will come back to you," even though God had told him to offer his son as a burnt offering.

Abraham was "fully convinced that what He had promised He was also able to perform" (Romans 4:21). God "gives life to the dead and calls those things which do not exist as though they did" (Romans 4:17). Abraham had faith that God, the Creator of all things, could follow through on His promise. When we know whose we are and who we are in Him, we are able to declare what God has purposed for our lives in spite of our present conditions.

Romans 4:18 says that Abraham, "contrary to hope, in hope believed, so that he became the father of many nations, according to what was spoken, 'So shall your descendants be.'" Abraham maintained his expectation that God would fulfill His promises, despite the age of his body and the task given him to offer his son as a sacrifice. Abraham's faith did not waver. He told his servants that both he and his son would return.

The faith test prepares you for the future and shows you whether you love the vision more than you love God. The test will be different for each person, but the process of the test will show you something about yourself before you can move forward.

The Test of Sacrifice

In order to fulfill God's purpose for you, you must be prepared to lose everything. You have to be willing to give God your life, your dreams, and your expectations. Abraham was willing to give God his beloved son, the son of the promise, and trust Him to work everything out according to His will.

Abraham gathered the materials he would need for the sacrifice and set off with his son (Genesis 22:6). Isaac asked, "Look, the fire and the wood, but where is the lamb for a burnt offering?" (Genesis 22:7). Abraham replied, "My son, God will provide for Himself the lamb for a burnt offering" (Genesis 22:8). Abraham spoke the words of faith, no matter how grim the situation seemed. No matter where you are in your life, you always need to have God's words in your heart.

God wants your best, not your leftovers. We worship God by giving Him our lives. We demonstrate our love for Him when we offer Him our best. Are you willing to sacrifice what you love most in order to fulfill what God has for you? When you obey God, He gives you strength, power, and blessings that enable you to do what you never would have done on your own.

If you surrender completely to God and follow His direction in obedience and faith, then He will release what He has promised to you, in spite of your mistakes. He will give you true blessings that surpass anything you could achieve on your own.

Exchange the Old for the New

You may sense God leading you in a specific direction, only to find that the plan has changed. We have to be ready to transition in the middle of the road. God stopped Abraham just before he sacrificed his son (Genesis 22:10–12). Abraham had made the preparations, but he wasn't meant to follow that exact plan all the way through.

We can't afford to allow the motions and routines to cause us to forget the mission. The everyday patterns, worries, and distractions of life can cause complacency, stagnation, and a lack of growth, which is death (Luke 8:11–15). It's time to shift to a higher level of faith!

The Lord is about to bring you into a new place and

change your reality completely. He will elevate you to a different space, where you may have to meet new people, enhance your skills, or learn another language. Some of your old habits and friends might not be able to come with you to this new reality.

The old mindset can't come with you because your mind needs to expand for where you are going. You need to reject bad habits and instill new, good habits. You need to remove yourself from activities that may hinder your progress. Instead of wasting time, you need to maximize your time to get the most out of each day.

You need to associate with people who have a heart for God's purpose and who want you to move toward your dream. Pursuing your dream means that you will have to disassociate yourself from certain people and places if you are going to turn your dream into reality.

God Will Provide

Hudson Taylor wrote, "God's work done in God's way will never lack God's provision."[11] God freely offers substitutes. We may not always see how or what He will provide, but He will come through in the right way and at the right time.

When Isaac started to question his father about what they would sacrifice, Abraham could not yet see God's provision. In that moment, Abraham may have been weak and fearful, but he stayed with what God had told him to do. Abraham said to his servants, "Stay here with the donkey; the lad and I will go yonder and worship, and we will come back to you" (Genesis 22:5). He was going to a place to meet God, a place where he could find clarity, direction, and confirmation.

Abraham needed God to speak to his heart and not to his head. Fear comes to our minds through thoughts that are contrary to our purposes, but faith in our hearts can overcome the fear. Abraham was able to speak words of faith from his heart, and because of his worship, fear was abandoned. This is why he was able to continue following God's instructions of sacrificing his son of the promise as an offering to the Lord.

Even though Abraham didn't know exactly what would happen, he still said in faith, "My son, God will provide..." (Genesis 22:8). He didn't give in to fear or doubt, and, just in time, God showed him the ram. It is right on the cusp of a breakthrough that many give up, but if you stick to your faith, God will provide. When you see the vision of God, understand the mission of God, and know the voice of God, you can declare His promises faithfully and trust that He will uphold you.

Don't you know that God has already provided for you? He has given you the resources for the vision. It's all there already. Listen to Him. Trust Him. Soon you will be able to see what He sees—that your provision has already been released.

WORKBOOK

Chapter Seven Questions

Question: What precious gifts has God given you? Have you, in faith, submitted them back to His direction and plan? Are you willing to sacrifice what you love in order to obey Him?

_____
_____
_____
_____
_____
_____
_____
_____
_____
_____

Question: Do you listen for God's voice? Do you know it when you hear it? What are some ways in which you can grow in sensitivity to God's voice?

Action Step: Make a list of the people and things that are important to you. Next to each one, write how you will actively commit that part of your life to God. At the bottom of the list, write out your commitment to keep trusting God for the perfect fulfillment of His purpose for your life.

Chapter Seven Notes

PART THREE:
Discovery of Your Gifts, Purpose, and Dream

CHAPTER EIGHT

Living Your Dream

Some people crawl out of bed in the morning, stretch, and then wonder what to do next. The list of options runs through their heads. It takes a while to decide that, yes, getting dressed is important. But what to wear? After a trip to the bathroom and a last-minute decision to shower, they wander to the closet and fuss over this and that item. Since they don't know what the day has in store, it's impossible to know how to dress.

Once they have clothes, they need to decide what to eat. Opening cupboards reveals options, but nothing sounds great. What about the diner in town? Yeah, maybe that. After eating, they figure that they may as well check out that shop down the road. Then they go to another store to grab a single item they'd noticed was missing from the cupboard. Traffic is terrible, so it takes longer than expected.

Before they know it, most of the day is gone, taken up by unimportant tasks and bouts of indecision. They go about their days aimlessly, and then they wonder why their lives don't seem meaningful.

Let's look in on a person who lives purposefully. He slaps the alarm clock off and rolls out of bed. He showers because he knows that it wakes him up fast, and then he feels fresh and ready for the day. Dressing is easy because he laid out his clothes the night before. He looks at his calendar and sees that there will be a meeting with his pastor, followed by work, then time with his family in the evening.

He packs a bag for the day, which includes a lunch, his Bible, and a book he's been reading. After meeting with his pastor and praying at church, he drives straight to work. By the time half the day has passed, he has accomplished a solid amount of work.

That's just one example of living on purpose. There are many other parts of our lives we must move forward with intention, especially if we're to obtain the dream God has for us.

The Dream Is Bigger Than You

God made Abraham an extravagant promise. He vowed that Abraham would become a great nation and that all of the families of the earth would be blessed through him (Genesis 12:1–3). That seemed like an unlikely promise, even an impossible one, since Abraham and Sarah were advanced in years, and Sarah had never been able to have children.

In order to walk into God's promise, Abraham had to do something he had never done before. He moved forward with the vision God gave him, leaving behind the security of family, friendship, and all he was familiar with to go to an unknown place. He stepped out in faith and followed God's perfect plan, which shaped his life for the good of all. God gave Abraham the gift of faith, which he certainly needed over the years, and Abraham exercised the gift regularly (Romans 4:16–22; Hebrews 11:8–19).

Isaac was born to Abraham and Sarah as a result of God's covenant promise (Genesis 21:1–3). God's instruction for Abraham to sacrifice his son was the test that demonstrated Abraham's reverence for God and his confidence in God's faithfulness to keep His promise.

Abraham prepared to offer up his son as a sacrifice, having the assurance that God would make a way where there seemed to be no way. Covenant love provided a timely sacrifice in place of Isaac. Centuries later, God's covenant love would provide another sacrifice on a mountain, where He would give His only Son as a blood sacrifice for all of mankind (John 3:16). Abraham's vision extended beyond his own life. His purpose was part of God's larger plan, and the same is true of you.

You Were Chosen

> *His divine power has given us everything we need for a godly life through our knowledge of him who called us by his own glory and goodness.*
> —*2 Peter 1:3 (NIV)*

God chose you with a plan in mind. He chose you before the creation of the world. He had you in His heart before He created the earth. He knew everything you would do. He knew that you would make some bad choices and do some ridiculous things, but He would love you anyway.

Even though God gave us the ability to make choices, His intended purpose for creating us still stands true today:

> *Blessed be the God and Father of our Lord Jesus Christ, who has blessed us with every spiritual blessing in the heavenly places in Christ, just as He chose us in Him before the foundation of the world, that we should be holy and without blame before Him in love, having predestined us to adoption as sons by Jesus Christ to Himself, according to the good pleasure of His will, to the praise of the glory of His grace, by which He made us accepted in the Beloved.*
> —*Ephesians 1:3-6*

God designed us to fulfill His purposes for the advancement of His kingdom on earth. What He intended from the beginning has never wavered. Your purpose has already been determined by God, and He has provided everything you need to fulfill it.

Finding Your Purpose

There is a natural desire inside each person's spirit to live out the purpose for which God created him or her. Many who are not listening to God's call for their lives find themselves sad, frustrated, and depressed. God wants you to live your life by faith and for His glory. Ephesians 5:10 says, "Figure out what will please Christ, and then do it" (MSG).

God is not forcing you to discover your purpose or find your gifts. It's your responsibility to find your purpose, and when you do find it, to pursue it intentionally and with faith:

> An unintentional life accepts everything and does nothing. An intentional life embraces only the things that will add to the mission of significance. Only by managing my thinking and shifting my thoughts from desire to deeds would I be able to bring about positive change. I needed to go from wanting to doing.[12]
> —**John C. Maxwell**

The following two chapters are designed to assist you with discovering your purpose and gifts. Even if you already know your purpose and gifts, I still encourage you to go through the process of discovery. I guarantee that you will rediscover some things about yourself, and your life will never be the same!

WORKBOOK

Chapter Eight Questions

Question: Do you tend to cruise through life or live with purpose? Do you see your life as meaningful?

Further Study: Read one chapter of the book of Proverbs a day according to the calendar date. Jot down verses that contain words such as *plan, direct, guide, purpose,* and *gift.* Consider these verses collectively. What do they teach about intentional living?

_____
_____
_____
_____
_____
_____
_____
_____
_____
_____

Action Step: For one week, keep track of all of your time in half-hour segments. Then chart how much time on average you spend at work, on entertainment, with other people, at church, in prayer, doing chores, and so forth. Are you living intentionally? In what areas could you improve? Selecting one area at a time, begin a focused campaign of intentional living.

Chapter Eight Notes

CHAPTER NINE

Discovering Your Purpose

Every person in the world was born with purpose. Everyone has a specific assignment to fulfill in a specific place, and this mission is meant to be accomplished within a specific time. Every person has the capacity to accomplish something great and make a significant impact in his or her area of influence. No matter who you are or where you are from, you were born with purpose.

Purpose is the reason for which something is done or created or for which something exists. The Greek word for *purpose* is *prothesis* (PROTH-uh-seez). *Pro-* means "before," and *thesis* refers to a place. If you take the parts together, the word means "setting forth," suggesting a deliberate plan, a proposition, an advance plan, or an intentional design.[13]

Many people wonder what their purpose is in life and how they can find it. In Scripture, God supplies the essentials for discovering our purpose. Chapters 1 and 2 of Genesis reveal man's intended purpose and value, as he is a special creation of God. At some point in life, we all hunger for meaning and purpose. We feel deep within that we matter and can make a difference.

Please understand this: God would not have allowed you to start your life unless your purpose had been established in eternity. Jeremiah 1:5 says, "Before I formed you in the womb I knew you, before you were born I set you apart; I appointed you as a prophet to the nations" (NIV). The key word is "before." Your purpose was already determined before you were born. You have been set apart and appointed to fulfill a specific assignment to a specific group of people in a certain place in the world.

Your life did not just happen by chance; it is the divine design of God. You were not born to go through life aimlessly, without any direction or focus. If you don't try to discover your purpose, there's a strong possibility that you will spend your life doing the wrong things. God has so much more for you. To live life as God intended, you must discover your purpose, the reason for your existence.

Steps for Moving Forward

The process of discovering your purpose starts with seeking God through prayer. People of purpose are people of prayer. Genesis 12:1 begins, "Now the LORD had said to Abram…." The word "said" indicates that there was an exchange of words, a conversation, between God and Abraham. This verse is also an indication of prayer. In its simplest form, prayer means to listen and talk. (Other passages that indicate Abraham's prayer life include Genesis 12:7–8, 13:3–4, 13:14–17, 15, and 18:16–33).

The second step is to schedule some time to work

through the following questions. You should schedule a few hours to be alone, maybe setting aside some time on the weekend or even taking a day off from work.

It's easy to be overwhelmed as you start looking for your purpose, so take your time and be honest with yourself as you answer the questions. Keep in mind that your purpose is about your entire life, not just a piece of it, so don't rush through the process.

You need to be diligent and honest as you answer these questions. Looking at your past and present experiences can provide insight into how your life has shaped you for your purpose.

1. What are your three greatest talents?
2. What is your greatest character strength?
3. What would your peers say you are good at doing?
4. What have your life experiences prepared you to do?
5. What is your greatest passion—in other words, the thing you love doing so much that you would gladly do it for free?
6. What is so important to you that you would be willing to die for it?

Some people look at their current circumstances and become discouraged because they are not where they want to be. However, looking at the present is part of the process of discovering your purpose and realizing your dreams. Answer the following questions to help you see the potential of the present.

1. What are your current resources? (Include time, money, personal connections, knowledge, and skills.)
2. What current circumstances can you change to free up more resources to create more opportunities?
3. What is unique about your current circumstances, your place in history, where you live, where you work, and the people you know?

Are you beginning to see the pattern of your past and present life and how they are shaping you for your future? Now it's time to ask yourself questions as you look to the future.

1. If you could be anything you wanted, what would you be?
2. If you could bring healing to a problem in the world, what would it be?
3. If you were to die tomorrow, how would you want to be remembered?
4. What would your legacy be?

When you have identified something you are passionate about, you have found a clue to your purpose. Now you can work out the specifics of your purpose by doing something with the information you've gained through this process of discovery.

Calling and Purpose

I remember a time in my life when I believed that God spoke to me about giving up something dear to my heart. I had started a ministry to men in 1991. I prayed about, studied, and practiced the principles of manhood and Christlikeness. I trained men to lead men's ministry in churches, and I taught young men in schools and prisons how to prepare for manhood.

I also coordinated regional men's conferences for one of the largest men's ministries in America. The ministry to which I was called had the potential to become a major ministry to men worldwide. However, I sensed the Lord leading me to let it go. It took me a while, but eventually I gave it up because I love God more than anything. It was then that I learned that my life is about His purpose.

The ministry to men wasn't my purpose. It was the tool God used to shape my character for His purpose. The call of God on my life is to be an example for believers by leading a Christlike, Christ-centered life at home, in my community, in my church, in my city, in this nation, and throughout the world.

My mission is to lead people to inherit their promises from God. As He said to Joshua:

> *Every place that the sole of your foot will tread upon I have given you, as I said to Moses. ... Be strong and of good*

> *courage, for to this people you shall divide as an inheritance the land which I swore to their fathers to give them.*
> —*Joshua 1:3, 6*

    This inheritance is not only a material or geographical possession, but physical and spiritual as well. The promise of obtaining the inheritance goes back to the covenant God made with Abraham in Genesis 12:1–3. Therefore, my purpose is the same as my call, which is to be an example of Christlikeness as a man, minister, and leader and to encourage, educate, and equip people with discovering their identity and purpose. My purpose is to help other people find their gifts, maximize their leadership potential, realize their God-given dreams, and implement the vision God has given them for their personal lives and ministry.

    Your calling could be different from your purpose. You may be called to be a doctor, with the purpose of winning souls. You may be called to be a minister, but your purpose may be to minister to the widows in a nursing home. You may be called to be an entrepreneur, but your purpose may be to equip and mentor others, teaching them how to develop and establish a business for supporting Kingdom work.

    Do you see the difference? Your calling is the task you have been given, while your purpose is the mission to which the task contributes. Your responsibility is to discover your purpose and be obedient to the call of God.

    Don't worry if you don't have the full picture right now. You have to start somewhere to get someplace. You may not yet know exactly what you should be doing, but if you undertake this process of discovery, you will have a foundation on which to begin building a purposeful and meaningful life that will have a positive impact on this generation and generations to come.

WORKBOOK

Chapter Nine Questions

Question: In your own words, explain the difference between a person's purpose and his or her calling. Can you think of an example of how these are different in your own life or the life of someone you know?

_____

_____

_____

_____

_____

_____

_____

Further Study: Read the passages in Genesis that show interactions between Abraham and God. How would you describe Abraham's prayer life, and what can you learn from it? Why is prayer so important to finding your purpose? Do you have a consistent prayer life? If not, what steps will you take to make prayer a priority?

Action Step: Set aside time to work through the questions in this chapter. From your answers, write a concise purpose statement for your life. This is just a starting point. You can make changes to your statement as you learn and grow. What initial steps can you take as you allow God to unfold your purpose?

Chapter Nine Notes

CHAPTER TEN

Your Gift, Your Responsibility

Every person has a unique set of gifts, talents, abilities, power, and opportunities to accomplish great things in life. The key to living an effective life on purpose is to discover your gifts, learn how to use them, and channel them in the right direction.

Understanding Your Gifts

Understanding your spiritual gifts and strengths is vital to developing your personal plan for growth and maturity as you pursue your God-given purpose, dreams, and visions. A spiritual gift is an expression of the Holy Spirit in the lives of believers that empowers them to serve in the capacity of their purpose and calling. Spiritual gifts have been provided to equip believers to glorify God for the advancement of the Kingdom of God to the lost, broken, and downtrodden with the gospel of Jesus Christ.

A strength, on the other hand, is a group of your greatest talents linked to what you do best. Your greatest areas of talent are likely sources of potential strengths. Each person naturally has a group of talents. Your specific set of talents is a major part of what makes you a unique person, and that uniqueness holds great value for you and those around you.

A talent is available to every person, whether he or she is a believer or not, but only believers in Christ have spiritual gifts that benefit other believers and help in reaching unbelievers. Natural talents and spiritual gifts are closely related. A person with musical talent may also have the spiritual gift of encouragement. This person can use music to encourage and inspire people to grow closer to the Lord.

The Bible is more specific on spiritual gifts than natural talents and abilities (Romans 12:6–8; 1 Corinthians 12–14; Ephesians 4:7–16; 1 Peter 4:10–11).[14]

Below are definitions of the gifts of the Spirit:[15]

> **Apostle:** An apostle is "one sent forth."[16] A true apostle is always one with a commission. The church sends apostles from the body to plant churches or be missionaries (Acts 13:1–5; 1 Corinthians 12:28; Ephesians 2:19–22, 4:11). An apostle's ministry embraces all other ministry gifts.
>
> **Prophet:** A prophet speaks by divine inspiration. He delivers an immediate revelation, which is not something he thought of, but something given at the spur of the moment by sudden inspiration of the Holy Spirit. There is a significant difference between prophesying and the ministry of the prophet.
>
> **Evangelist:** The word evangelist occurs only three times in the New Testament. The evangelist brings the message of the redeeming grace of God. His favorite theme is

salvation in its simplest form. This gift builds the church by winning souls (Ephesians 4:11).

Pastor: The word pastor literally means "shepherd."[17] The pastor is the under-shepherd. He is the head and overseer of the flock and/or church group (Ephesians 4:11; Acts 20:28; 1 Peter 5:1–4). A person called to this office is connected to the heart of God and is married to the church.

Teacher: Teachers are gifted to keep an eye on and instruct people in the revealed truth of God's Word, regardless of public office (Romans 12:7; 1 Corinthians 12:28; Ephesians 4:11).

Prophecy: Prophecy is the supernatural capacity to expound truth from God, without explanation. To prophesy, one operates in the gift of prophecy, speaking "edification and exhortation and comfort to men" (1 Corinthians 14:3). Prophecy can also convict the unbeliever of the reality of God.

Ministry/service/helps: This describes the supernatural ability to recognize practical needs in the body of Christ and joyfully give assistance to meeting those needs (Romans 12:7; 1 Corinthians 12:28).

Exhortation: Exhortation refers to the spiritual capacity to move believers forward in their walk with the Lord, especially in times of personal distress, by encouraging and comforting them or the church (Romans 12:8).

Giving: Giving (Romans 12:8) is the supernatural ability to contribute to the emotional and/or physical support of others. It also includes the gift of financial means to support the advancement of the gospel of Christ.

Leadership: Leadership is the God-given capacity to lead effectively in all areas of life and to motivate people to work together in unity to accomplish the purposes of the church. A person gifted in this way may serve in administration or even as a deacon (Philippians 1:1; Romans 12:8).

Mercy: Mercy is the God-given ability to feel and express genuine empathy and compassion in a cheerful and practical manner to people experiencing personal distress (Romans 12:8).

Word of wisdom: A word of wisdom refers to a spiritual utterance at a given moment that, through the Holy Spirit, supernaturally discloses the mind, purpose, and way of God as applied to a specific situation, question, answer, or fact (1 Corinthians 12:8).

Word of knowledge: This describes the supernatural revelation of information—past, present, or future facts—pertaining to a person or an event given for a specific purpose, usually having to do with an immediate need (1 Corinthians 12:8).

Faith: The gift of faith (1 Corinthians 12:9) goes beyond natural and saving faith. It supernaturally trusts and does not doubt with reference to the specific matters involved. It visualizes the will of God before it becomes true in one's experience.

Healing: Healing is the supernatural ability of the Holy Spirit to heal many sicknesses, diseases, and disorders of the mind, body, and soul (1 Corinthians 12:9).

Miracles: A miracle is the manifestation of power beyond the ordinary course of natural law. It is the sovereignty of God clearly displayed. The gift of miracles is a divine enablement to do something that bypasses natural means to accomplish an act or goal (1 Corinthians 12:10).

Discerning of spirits: Discernment is the God-given ability to discern the spirit world and to detect motives and the true source of circumstances (1 Corinthians 12:10).

Different kinds of tongues: The gift of tongues is the supernatural ability to speak a language unknown to the speaker. The plural refers to different forms of tongues (known spoken languages of Acts 2:4–11) and unknown utterances designed particularly for praying and singing in the Spirit, mostly for private worship (1 Corinthians 12:10; 14:2, 14:4, 14:6–19).

Interpretation of tongues: Interpretation is the gift of translating a message of the Spirit to others, especially when exercised in public (1 Corinthians 12:10, 14:5, 14:13). (It is not the translation of a foreign language.)

Administration: Administration is a refined form of the gift of leadership, with the ability to manage the details necessary to implement the short-range and long-term projects and goals of the body of Christ (1 Corinthians 12:28).

Use It or Lose It

Jesus told a powerful parable about our responsibility to use what God gives us (Matthew 25:14–30). In the story, a wealthy man was about to travel to a faraway country, so he called in his servants to make arrangements. The master divided his goods among his servants, allocating the talents, a form of money in ancient Israel, according to how skilled the servants were. He gave five talents to one servant, two talents to another servant, and one talent to a third servant. Then the master left on his journey.

The servant who had five talents traded with them, using his business skills, and received five more talents. The servant who had two talents invested them and made two more. The third servant, who received one talent, buried the money, afraid that he would lose it.

When the master returned, he checked on his servants. The servant who had been given five talents brought his master ten. The master was delighted and praised him, saying, "Well done, good and faithful servant; you were faithful over a few things, I will make you ruler over many things. Enter into the joy of your lord" (Matthew 25:21).

The second servant brought in four talents, two more than he'd been given, and the wealthy man was pleased. He gave the second servant the same praise as he had given the first.

The master's response to the third servant's choice was not so favorable:

> Then he who had received the one talent came and said, "Lord, I knew you to be a hard man, reaping where you have not sown, and gathering where you have not scattered seed. And I was afraid, and went and hid your talent in the ground. Look, there you have what is yours."
>
> But his lord answered and said to him, "You wicked and lazy servant, you knew that I reap where I have not sown, and gather where I have not scattered seed. So you ought to have deposited my money with the bankers, and at my coming I would have received back my own with interest. So take the talent from him, and give it to him who has ten talents.
>
> "For to everyone who has, more will be given, and he will have abundance; but from him who does not have, even what he has will be taken away."
> —**Matthew 25:24–29**

When we are given talents, skills, and gifts, it's our responsibility to do something with them. The consequences of not using them are disastrous for us. Our gifts are given to us with the intent of helping us to fulfill our assignments. If we use our gifts, talents, and abilities correctly, we are guaranteed success.

Your Gift Is the Key to Success

Most people perceive success to look like the wealth of Bill Gates, the athletic ability of LeBron James, the entrepreneurship of Bishop T.D. Jakes, the songwriting skills of Jay-Z, or the vision of Harriet Tubman. Many people think that success means looking like some other person, but the truth is that if you try to be like someone other than yourself, you won't be successful.

What is success? Success isn't the same for any two people because all of us are created to be different and unique. However, the process is the same for everyone because the process is based on principles that don't change.

I have adopted a working definition of success developed by one of my mentors, John Maxwell: "Success is knowing your purpose in life, growing to reach your maximum potential, and adding value or making a difference in the lives of others."[18] When you incorporate this definition into your life, you are not just becoming a success, you are successful!

Faith and Success

Let's take another look at the beginning of Jesus' parable about the servants entrusted with their master's wealth:

> *For the kingdom of heaven is like a man traveling to a far country, who called his own servants and delivered his*

> *goods to them. And to one he gave five talents, to another two, and to another one, to each according to his own ability; and immediately he went on a journey.*
> —*Matthew 25:14–15*

Notice that each person is given talents according to his ability. Ability means power. Faith gives us the ability, or the power, to develop our gifts and talents. However, we need faith to receive and activate these gifts, talents, and abilities. They won't start working properly and as intended until we use our faith.

Romans 12:3 says that "God has dealt to each one a measure of faith." The measure may be different for every person, just as the spiritual gifts, talents, and abilities are different for every person. What we do with that measure of faith will determine the growth of our faith.

Even though society tells us that with a good education, we can become very successful in life, education alone is not enough to activate your talents and use them to the fullest potential. It's your faith that will activate those abilities. Faith will give you the power to fulfill the purpose God has for your life.

Stir Up Your Gifts

It is your responsibility to discover and activate your gifts. Paul wrote to Timothy, "Therefore I remind you to stir up the gift of God which is in you through the laying on of my hands" (2 Timothy 1:6). If there was nothing there, why would Paul tell Timothy to stir it up? Every person was born with gifts and abilities to use for the purpose he or she was created to fulfill.

So, stir it up! The more you fan the flame, the bigger the fire will grow. God has given everyone the right tools and opportunities to work with, so don't let what He gives you go to waste. Activate and develop your gifts by putting your faith into action.

Pray this prayer aloud:

> Father, just as Paul told Timothy to stir the gift that was in him, I want to stir the gifts You have placed in me. I want my gifts to be used for Your glory. I want to use those gifts to bring fulfillment to my life. I will confess in faith that I've been born at the right time to accomplish the vision You have given me. Father, I thank You for the gifts You placed in me. Holy Spirit, reveal my gifts. I don't want a mediocre life. Teach me how to use my gifts with confidence and help me to walk in purpose each day of my life. I will exercise my gifts with joy and perseverance in the name of Jesus. Amen.

WORKBOOK

Chapter Ten Questions

Question: How can you develop your specific gift(s)? Why is it important to activate your gift(s) in faith, regardless of your education and skills?

_____
_____
_____
_____
_____
_____
_____
_____
_____
_____
_____

Further Study: Study the parable of the talents in Matthew 25:14–30. What can you learn from this story about responsibility, initiative, and accountability? How are you doing in each of those areas?

_____

_____

_____

_____

_____

_____

_____

_____

_____

_____

Action Step: Talk to leaders you know who are clearly operating in their gifts and ask them how they discovered their gifts, how they stepped out in faith to activate them, and how doing so has impacted their lives. What can you learn from them?

Chapter Ten Notes

CONCLUSION

Release What God Has for You

God told Abraham to leave the familiar—his father's house, his country—so that God could show him something new. God promised Abraham that he would be blessed and a blessing to many people. At that time, Abraham was surely filled with fear and doubt, but his willingness to step out in obedience took his faith to another level.

Even though he was only partially obedient in the beginning of his journey and fear of the unknown was always present, Abraham eventually won in life because he was willing to learn and to put his faith in God. He listened to God and ultimately reached his full potential.

God's purpose for your life is for you to win! However, in order to win, you have to know your purpose. You must have a clear picture of who you are and where you are going. As E. Paul Hovey observed, "A blind man's world is bounded by the limits of his touch; an ignorant man's world by the limits of his knowledge; a great man's world by the limits of his vision."[19]

God has given you a vision for your life. This purposed dream will require you to leave your comfort zone and trust God to provide for you as you step forward in faith. You need to keep the vision in front of you always. The obstacles on your path will either knock you off course or reveal who you really are and shape you for your purpose.

Don't stop. Don't quit. This is not the time to give in. Keep pressing toward the upward call on your life. Your purpose has already been decided by God. You need only to discover it and obey Him.

The most important factor in turning your dream into reality is making prayer your priority. It is in that place of faithful submission and intimate conversation that God will reveal His purpose for you and provide you with the clarity and strength to pursue it.

In the words of Dr. Edwin Louis Cole, "Dreams are the substance of great achievements."[20] When you know God's purpose for you and embrace the vision He gives you, then you can pray effectively to turn your dream into reality. Your prayers may not manifest in a day, but it's what you continue to do in faith every day that brings the dream into reality.

About the Author

Melvin L. Taylor Jr. serves the City of Buffalo as the senior pastor at the New Life World Harvest Restoration Center. A motivational speaker, lecturer, leadership consultant, and businessman, he is the founder and CEO of MLT Leadership, Inc., and the Eleven Twenty-Four Real Estate Group.

Melvin encourages, equips, and empowers leaders to serve in their spheres of influence with excellence. He desires to celebrate the presence of God in worship and to communicate what he has learned from his personal experience and from proven leaders who have made a significant impact on his life.

In over twenty-five years of leading and equipping individuals and teams, Melvin has collaborated with leaders and organizations nationally and internationally to achieve the highest level of effectiveness and improve leadership accountability and productivity. His devotion to the Word of God has motivated him to continue earning his degree in Christian Leadership and Education at Regent University.

Melvin is happily married to and in love with "his wife for life," Pamela Taylor, who has served faithfully with him in his endeavors to inspire people to turn their God-given dreams into reality.

REFERENCES

Notes

[1] Strong, James. "H8646 – Terach." In *Strong's Exhaustive Concordance of the Bible* (Hunt & Eaton, 1894), quoted in Blue Letter Bible. https://www.blueletterbible.org/lang/lexicon/lexicon.cfm?Strongs=H8646&t=KJV.

[2] Munroe, Myles. Quoted in "'The Wealthiest Place on Earth Is the Cemetery' and Other Memorable Myles Munroe Quotes," The Cable (November 10, 2014). https://www.thecable.ng/wealthiest-place-earth-cemetery---memorable-munroe-quotes.

[3] Mensah, Benjamin Y. *The Believer's Companion*. Xlibris, 2010, p. 37.

[4] "The Difference Between Faith and Belief." New Creeations. https://newcreeations.org/the-difference-between-faith-and-belief/.

[5] "The Difference Between Faith and Belief."

[6] Strong, James. "H3876– Lowt." In *Strong's Exhaustive Concordance of the Bible* (Hunt & Eaton, 1894), quoted in Blue Letter Bible. https://www.blueletterbible.org/lang/lexicon/lexicon.cfm?Strongs=H3876&t=KJV.

[7] Strong's H2377 – chazown." In *Strong's Exhaustive Concordance of the Bible* (Hunt & Eaton, 1894), quoted in Blue Letter Bible. https://www.blueletterbible.org/lang/lexicon/lexicon.cfm?t=kjv&strongs=h2377.

[8] Aesop. "The Hare and the Tortise." *Aesop for Children.* In Read.gov, Library of Congress. http://www.read.gov/aesop/025.html.

[9] Leaf, Caroline. *Think, Learn, Succeed: Understanding and Using Your Mind to Thrive at School, the Workplace, and Life.* Baker Books, 2018.

[10] Maxwell, John C. *The Success Journey: The Process of Living Your Dreams.* Thomas Nelson, 1997.

[11] Pettengill, Mike. "God's Work, God's Way." The Gospel Coalition. May 21, 2015. https://www.thegospelcoalition.org/article/gods-work-gods-way.

[12] Maxwell, John C. *Intentional Living: Choosing a Life That Matters.* Center Street, 2015.

[13] See G4286 in *The New Strong's Exhaustive Concordance*; *Vine's Complete Expository Dictionary of Old and New Testament Words*; and "Word Wealth" (Romans 8:28), *The Spirit-Filled Life Bible* (NKJV Version), Thomas Nelson, p. 1701.

[14] For more information on talents, see CliftonStrengths at www.strengthsquest.com.

[15] See Rick Yohn, *Discover Your Spiritual Gift and Use It* (Heritage Builders, 2011); Kenneth Kinghorn, *Gifts of the Spirit* (Abingdon, 1976).

[16] Hagin, Kenneth E. *The Ministry Gifts*. Faith Library Publications.

[17] See G4166 in *The New Strong's Exhaustive Concordance*; *Vine's Complete Expository Dictionary of Old and New Testament Words*.

[18] Maxwell, John. "What I Believe About Success." John C. Maxwell. March 5, 2014. https://www.johnmaxwell.com/blog/what-i-believe-about-success/.

[19] Maxwell, *The Success Journey*.

[20] Cole, Edwin Louis. *The Potential Principle: Living Your Life to Its Maximum*. Honor, 1984.

www.ingramcontent.com/pod-product-compliance
Lightning Source LLC
LaVergne TN
LVHW052341080426
835508LV00045B/3149